Contents

Some words are shown in bold, **like this**. You can find out what they mean by looking in the glossary.

Water for life

Plants, animals, and people are living things.
All living things need water to live.

Investigate

Water

Charlotte Guillain

www.heinemann.co.uk/library
Visit our website to find out more information about Heinemann Library books.

To order:
☎ Phone 44 (0) 1865 888066

▤ Send a fax to 44 (0) 1865 314091

▢ Visit the Heinemann Bookshop at www.heinemann.co.uk/library to browse our catalogue and order online.

Heinemann Library is an imprint of Pearson Education Limited,
a company incorporated in England and Wales having its
registered office at Edinburgh Gate, Harlow, Essex, CM20 2JE
– Registered company number: 00872828

Heinemann is a registered trademark of Pearson Education Ltd.
Text © Pearson Education Limited 2008
First published in hardback in 2008
Paperback edition first published in 2009
The moral rights of the proprietor have been asserted.

Edited by Sarah Shannon, Catherine...
Designed by Joanna Hinton-Malivoir...
    and Hart McLeod
Picture research by Liz Alexander and...
Production by Duncan Gilbert
Originated by Chroma Graphics (Overseas) Pte. Ltd
Printed and bound in China by Leo Paper Group

ISBN 978 0 431932 80 4 (hardback)
12 11 10 09 08
10 9 8 7 6 5 4 3 2 1
ISBN 978 0 431932 99 6 (paperback)
13 12 11 10 09
10 9 8 7 6 5 4 3 2 1

British Library Cataloguing in Publication Data
Guillain, Charlotte
   Water. - (Investigate)
   551.4'8
A full catalogue record for this book is available from the
British Library.

Acknowledgements
We would like to thank the following for permission to reproduce
photographs: ©Alamy pp. **5** (Stock Connection Distribution), **16**,
30 (D. Hurst), **19** (Digital Archive Japan); ©Corbis pp. **6** (Arctic-
... Smith), **13** (Matt Sullivan/Reuters), **15** (David
... ty Images pp. **8** (PhotoDisc), **10** (Image Bank), **18**
... (Steve Casmiro/Riser), **22** (Taxi), **23**, **28** (Stone), **26**,
... (Iconica); ©Istockphoto pp. **7** (Kent Metschan),
... ©Masterfile p. **14** (Daniel Barillot); ©Photolibrary p.
... ce Photo Library pp. **7** (Cordelia Molloy), **24** (Mike
... usa), **25** (Cape Grim B.A.P.S./Simon Fraser); ©Tips
... aymond Forbes).

...ph of waves rolling on a beach reproduced with
... Getty Images (Norbert Wu/Science Faction).

... been made to contact copyright holders of
... uced in this book. Any omissions will be rectified in
subsequent printings if notice is given to the publishers.

↓ People need to drink about 8 glasses of water a day.

More than half your body is water. People need to drink water to stay healthy. People also need water to wash themselves and to grow plants for food.

Bodies of water

Water is on Earth in bodies of water. There are different types of bodies of water.

1

Streams are the smallest bodies of water. They often flow into a river.

Water bubbles up through mountain springs and flows into streams.

2

Rivers are large, flowing bodies of water. They move water in one direction. ⬇

Lakes are large bodies of water with land all around them. Rivers can flow into lakes. ⬆

Q What are the largest bodies of water?

7

A Oceans are the largest bodies of water.

8

This map shows the five oceans of the world.

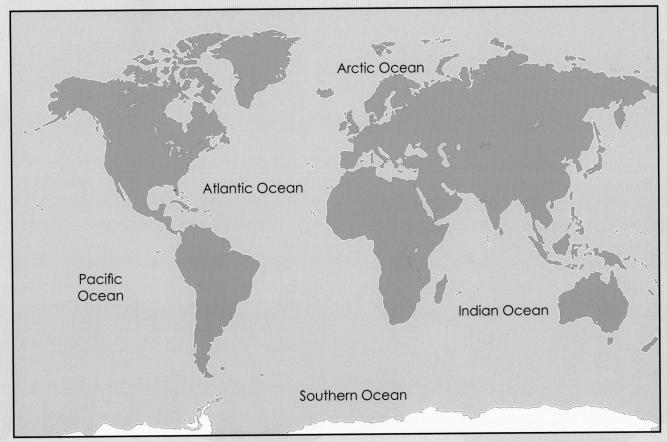

Arctic Ocean

Atlantic Ocean

Pacific
Ocean

Indian Ocean

Southern Ocean

OCEAN FACTS

➡ The Pacific Ocean is the largest ocean.

➡ Almost all of the water on Earth is salt water.
  It is found in the oceans.

9

Changing water

Most of the water in the ocean is **liquid**. The water we drink and wash with is liquid. Rainwater is liquid.

Q What happens when water gets very cold?

CLUES

- What happens when you put water into the freezer? Does it stay liquid?

- When do you see icicles?

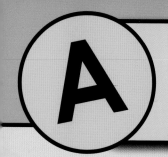

A When water gets very cold it **freezes**. Frozen water is **solid**.

Water freezes when the **temperature** is below 0°C (32°F). A **thermometer** measures the temperature.

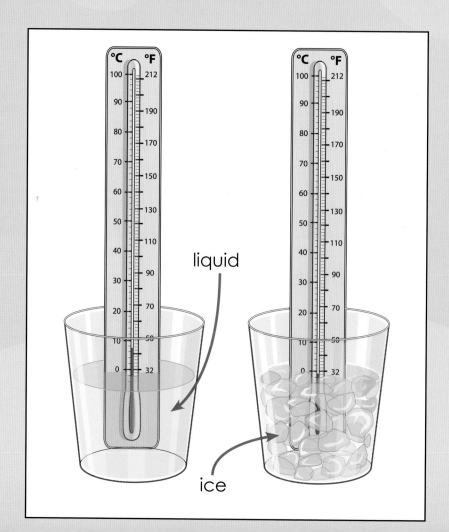

liquid

ice

Frozen water is called ice. Ice can be used to:

➠ keep food fresh

➠ keep drinks cold

➠ play sports such as skating and ice hockey

➠ make **sculptures**.

13

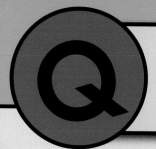

What happens when water gets warm?

14

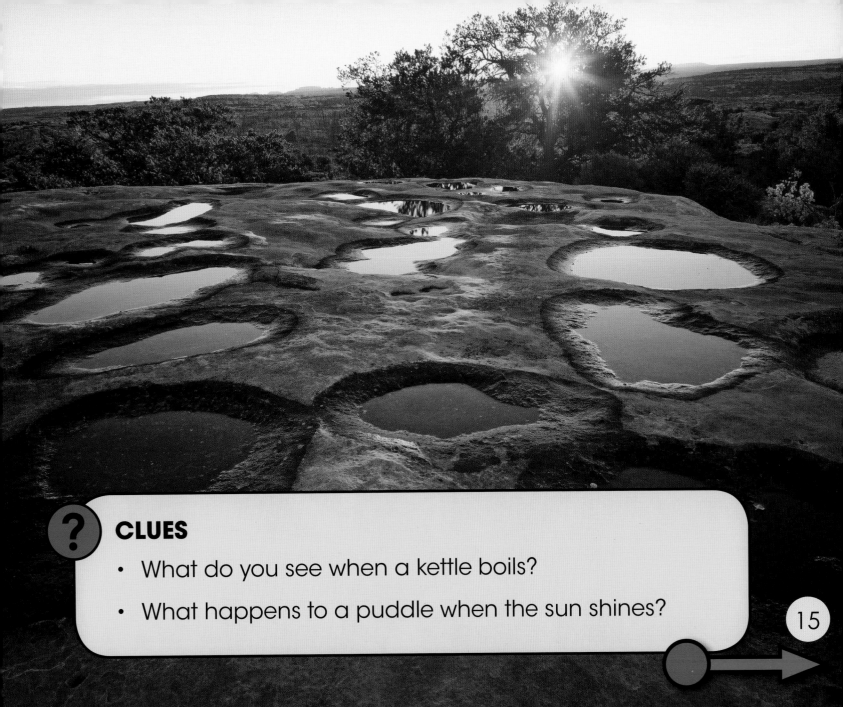

? **CLUES**

- What do you see when a kettle boils?

- What happens to a puddle when the sun shines?

15

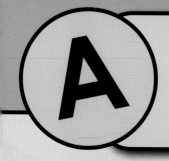

When water gets warm, it evaporates and becomes **water vapour**. When water gets very hot, it boils and becomes steam.

Water boils when the temperature is 100°C (212°F).
When water boils it turns from a liquid into a gas.
When water turns into a gas it **evaporates**. The water
vapour rises into the air.

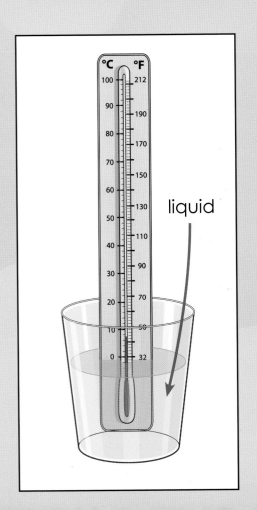

liquid

steam

The water cycle

What happens when the sun shines on a lake?

?

CLUES

- Does the sun make the water warmer or colder?

- What happens to water when it gets warm?

A When the sun shines on a lake, the water **evaporates**. The water becomes **water vapour** and rises into the air.

 Water vapour in the air makes clouds in the sky.

There are different types of clouds, including:

➡ Cumulus clouds. These look puffy. We can see these clouds on a sunny day. It might rain when there are cumulus clouds.

➡ Cirrus clouds. These look thin and wispy. They are found very high in the sky. It doesn't rain when there are only cirrus clouds in the sky.

➡ Stratus clouds. These stretch out in flat layers. There could be rain when there are stratus clouds.

➡ Cumulonimbus clouds. These are very large. There may be a storm where there are cumulonimbus clouds.

Q When the **temperature** cools, what happens to the clouds?

22

CLUE

- What happens when steam from a shower touches a cold mirror?

A When the temperature cools, water vapour turns to **liquid**. Steam turns to liquid when it hits a cold window or mirror. This is called **condensation**. When water vapour in a cloud cools, it rains. This is also called condensation.

People can use a **rain gauge** to measure how much rain has fallen. The rain gauge catches rainwater so people can measure it.

When it rains, the water falls back into rivers, lakes, and oceans. Water also falls on to the soil and goes into the ground.

Trees and plants get water from the soil through their roots. Plants need water and sunlight to live and grow.

People can also get water from under the ground. Many people get their water from underground wells. Other people get their water from rivers and lakes. The water travels through pipes to taps in people's houses.

The water we use has travelled a long way. It has gone from bodies of water to clouds and back again as rain. Trees, plants, and animals can only live on Earth because of water. Water is very important in our lives so we must not waste a tiny drop.

Checklist

Living things such as plants, animals, and people need water.

Water can be:

liquid

solid

gas

Bodies of water include:

➡ streams
➡ rivers
➡ lakes
➡ oceans.

Glossary

condensation when water vapour cools and turns back into a liquid

evaporate when liquid heats up and turns into a gas

freeze when a liquid cools and turns into a solid

gas substance like air that completely fills any container in which it is kept and has no shape of its own

liquid something that flows, such as water and oil

rain gauge a tool for measuring how much rain has fallen

sculpture a statue or carving

solid something which has a definite shape. Ice, wood, and stone are all solid.

temperature how hot or cold something is

thermometer a tool for measuring the temperature

water vapour water in the form of gas. Steam is water vapour.

Index